Great Sandwiches

A kitchen counter-top book of 100 recipes for old favorites, classics, crowd pleasers, party styles, and just plain comfort food sandwiches.

Great Sandwiches

Copyright © 2010 by JJT Media
Compiled by Joan Ashley
All Rights Reserved

ISBN 978-1451542448

Sandwiches, how we came to know them....

Although combinations of bread or pastry filled with meat or cheese and dressed with condiments have been enjoyed by many cultures, in many ways since ancient times, food historians generally attribute the creation of the sandwich, as we know it today, to John Montagu, 4th Earl of Sandwich. This Englishman was said to have been fond of gambling. As the story goes, in 1762, during a 24 hour gambling streak he requested the cook prepare his food in such a way that it would not interfere with his game. The cook presented him with sliced meat between two pieces of toast. It was perfect! This meal required no utensils and could be eaten with one hand, leaving the other free to continue the game.

In fact, Montague was not the originator of the sandwich, during his excursions in the Eastern Mediterranean, he enjoyed grilled pita breads and small canapés and sandwiches served by the Greeks and Turks and copied the concept for its obvious convenience.

None the less, sandwiches have become everyday fare, served as a PBJ for a youngster, tailgate extravaganzas for the Big Game, dainty finger canapés for an upscale social gathering. Everyone has a favorite! Here are 100 of those wonderfully satisfying convenient meals to choose from. Enjoy!!

Great Sandwiches

Contents

Page No.

Great Sandwiches

ADIRONDACK SANDWICHES

8 slices lean bacon
1/2 c. chopped onion
1 (16 oz.) can baked beans
2 tbsp. prepared chili sauce
1/4 c. creamy or chunky peanut butter
4 lg. slices whole grain bread, toasted
1/2 c. shredded Cheddar cheese

Preheat broiler. In a large skillet, over medium heat, cook the bacon until crisp; drain on paper towels. Pour off all but 1 tablespoon grease. Add onion; cook 2 minutes or just until tender. Stir in baked beans and chili sauce; heat through. Over low heat, stir in peanut butter; blend until smooth.

Spoon about 1/2 cup bean mixture onto each bread slice; top each with 2 bacon strips and 2 tablespoons cheese. Broil 6 inches from heat, 1-2 minutes or until cheese melts.

ARMENIAN SANDWICHES

2 lg. rounds Armenian cracker bread
3 tbsp. low-calorie mayonnaise
3 tbsp. Dijon-style mustard
2 oz. Neufchatel cream cheese, softened
1 c. sliced cucumber
1 c. sliced tomatoes
1 c. shredded leaf lettuce
2 tsp. herbal salt substitute

Place one cracker bread on a clean dampened dish towel. Spray the surface of the bread with a plant mister filled with water, until you can see a light glaze of water on the surface of the bread. Cover with another dampened towel, put the second cracker bread on top, mist that one and cover with two dampened towels. Every 10 minutes, remove towels, turn the breads over, mist them again, and replace the layers of towels. Repeat for 20 minutes or until crackers are soft enough to bend without tearing or cracking.

In a small bowl, combine the mayonnaise, mustard, and cream cheese. Spread a strip of this mixture across the center of one cracker bread. Place a row of cucumbers, tomatoes and lettuce on top of the spread, and sprinkle with herbal salt. Starting with the end closest to you, roll the bread tightly, as if rolling a sleeping bag. When you come to the edge of the bread, seal roll with an extra dab of cream cheese. Repeat with a second cracker bread. Place rolls seam-side down on counter; slice into 2-inch rounds. If you need to, secure each with a toothpick. Place on a plate and cover with plastic wrap until ready to serve. Makes 20 sandwiches, 5 servings.

BARBECUED BEEF FOR SANDWICHES

4 lb. beef roast
2 tbsp. vinegar
1 sm. bottle ketchup
2 c. celery, chopped
3 onions, chopped
1 tbsp. salt
2 tbsp. Worcestershire sauce
1 tbsp. chili powder
2 c. water

Mix ingredients together and pour over the roast. Bake in 275 to 325 degree oven for 5 hours or put into crock pot. Break apart or shred after it is cooked and pile it onto your favorite rolls or bread.

BARBECUED PORK SANDWICHES

2		Boneless pork loin roasts -- (2-1/2 to 3lb ea)
1	C	Water
2	tsp	Salt
2	C	Ketchup
2	C	Celery -- diced
1/3	c	Steak sauce
1/4	c	Brown sugar -- packed
1/4	c	Vinegar
2	tsp	Lemon juice
20		hamburger buns -- (20 to 25)

Place roasts in an 8-qt Dutch oven; add water and
  salt. Cover and cook on medium-low heat for 2-1/2
  hours or until meat is tender.
Remove roasts and shred with a fork; set aside.
  Skim fat from cooking liquid and discard.
  Drain all but 1 cup of the cooking liquid, add meat, ketchup, celery,
steak sauce, sugar, vinegar and lemon juice.
  Cover and cook over medium-low heat for 1-1/2 hours. Serve on
buns.

BAVARIAN BEEF SANDWICH

1 (8 oz)	pkg softened cream cheese
1/4 c	Sour cream
2 tbsp	Horseradish
12	Slices Rye bread **or**
6	Sub buns
	Lettuce
	Roast beef slices
6	Red onion slices

Combine cream cheese, sour cream, and horseradish, mixing until well blended. For each sandwich, spread bread with the the cream cheese mixture, add the meat, lettuce and onions. Add additional cream cheese spread if desired.

BEEF AND PORK TENDERLOIN SANDWICHES

| 1 | 6-7 lb | beef tenderloin, trimmed |
| 2 | 2-3 lb | pork tenderloins, trimmed |

Marinade:

1/2 cup	port wine
1/2 cup	brandy
1/2 tsp	dried tarragon leaves
1/2 tsp	dried whole thyme
2	bay leaves
1-1/4 tsp	salt
1/2 tsp	pepper
1/2 tsp	dry mustard
	Combine all ingredients in a small bowl, mixing well.

Vegetable oil
Party rye bread
Endive
Mayonnaise -- optional
Commercial barbecue sauce -- optional
prepared horseradish -- optional

*Marinate the beef and pork tenderloins together, but cook them separately.
Sandwiches can be prepared from either or both types of meat. Place tenderloins in a large pan or dish; pour marinade over top, and cover tightly. Refrigerate overnight, turning meat several times; drain. Place beef tenderloin, fat side up, on rack in a shallow roasting pan; rub with 1 tablespoon vegetable oil. Bake at 450 degrees for 15 minutes. Turn oven off; do not open door. Let roast remain in oven 45 minutes. (roast will be medium rare). Place pork tenderloins, fat side up, on rack in a shallow roasting pan; rub with 1 teaspoon vegetable oil. Bake at 325 degrees for 1 hour or until well done. Slice tenderloins, and place on serving platter.
Serve on party rye bread with endive; top with mayonnaise, barbecue sauce, or horseradish, if desired.

Yield: about 24 servings.

BEER - OX (Bierocks) SANDWICHES

For 12 Hoagie Rolls (serves 5-6). 2 1/2 lb. lean ground beef
1 med. size head cabbage, chopped fine
1 med. onion, chopped fine
2 tbsp. garlic powder
1 tbsp. crushed red pepper
Salt & pepper to taste
2 1/2 c. grated Cheddar cheese (optional)

Steam the cabbage and onion in a large covered pot for about 30 minutes. Cook the ground beef, garlic powder, and red pepper in a skillet until it changes color, add to the cabbage and cook for another 20 minutes. Season the mixture with salt and pepper to taste. Slice rolls lengthwise halfway through. Hollow out center of roll to form cup and stuff with meat mix, add cheese if desired, fold closed. Place on foil lined cookie sheet. Bake at 375 degrees until rolls are warm through and the cheese is melted.

BIG SANDWICH

Trim crusts from unsliced white or wheat bread. Cut loaf into four lengthwise slices, spread one side of each slice with softened butter.

--FIRST SLICE TOPPING:--
1 hard cooked egg, chopped
7 oz. can chopped shrimp
1/4 c. chopped celery
2 tsp. lemon juice
Dash salt & pepper
1/4 c. mayonnaise
Mix well. Spread on top of first slice of bread.

--SECOND SLICE TOPPING:--
3 oz. pkg. cream cheese
1 c. finely chopped pecans
9 oz. can well drained crushed pineapple
Mix well. Spread on top of second slice of bread.

--THIRD SLICE TOPPING:--
8 slices crisp bacon, crumbled
1 c. finely chopped, cooked chicken
1/4 c. mayonnaise
1 tbsp. chopped pimiento
Dash salt & pepper
Mix well. Spread on top of third slice of bread. Top with remaining slice and coat top and sides with the following frosting.

--FROSTING:--
2 (8 oz.) pkgs. softened cream cheese
1/2 c. half & half
Food coloring
Paper thin slices of cucumber

Mix cream cheese and half and half. Add food coloring to mixture (a delicate green). Garnish top with paper thin slices of cucumber overlapping the length of the loaf. Chill in refrigerator two or three hours. Serves 12 to 14.

CAJUN CHICKEN SANDWICHES

4	chicken breast halves without skin -- boneless
	powdered chipotle peppers -- to taste
2 tbsp	canola oil
4	hamburger buns

GARNISHES
chipotle pepper puree
thick sliced tomatoes
dill pickles
onion slices
lettuce leaves
cheese slices -- your choice
mustard
mayonnaise

Season the chicken breast halves. Heat the oil in a skillet. When oil is hot, place the chicken in the skillet & cook turning once or twice until chicken is done. Place chicken on a plate lined with paper towels to drain the oil.

Spread a little chipotle pepper puree on one half of each bun, on the other half spread your choice of mustard or mayonnaise. Place a piece of the chicken & any of the other garnishes you desire in the bun

CAJUN CUTLET SANDWICH

1/2 c. mayonnaise
1 tbsp. chopped fresh parsley
1 tsp. fresh lemon juice
1/2 tsp. grated lemon peel
1/2 tsp. salt
1/2 tsp. freshly ground pepper
1/2 tsp. cumin
1/4 tsp. paprika
1/8 tsp. ground red pepper
4 chicken cutlets, about 1/2" thick
3 tbsp. butter or margarine, melted
8 slices, about 1/2" thick, Italian
bread from lg. round loaf, toasted
4 lettuce leaves
8 thin slices red onion

Mix mayonnaise, parsley and lemon juice and peel in small bowl. Mix salt, pepper, cumin, paprika and red pepper in wide shallow bowl. Add chicken cutlets to spice mixture; turn to coat, then brush both sides with melted butter. Place in single layer on wax paper. Heat well seasoned large cast iron skillet over medium high heat just to smoking. Add half the cutlets and saute just until cooked through, 1-1/2 to 2 minutes per side. Transfer to plate and cover to keep warm. Repeat with remaining cutlets.

Spread 1 tablespoon lemon mayonnaise on each slice bread. Top 4 slices with lettuce leaf, 2 slices onion, chicken cutlet and second slice bread. Serve with potato salad.

CELEBRATION PICNIC SANDWICH

1 1/2 lb. round French bread
1/4 c. olive oil
2 cloves garlic, minced
3 lg. tomatoes, sliced
1/2 lb. assorted sliced luncheon meat
3 oz. sliced pepperoni or salami
1/4 lb. assorted sliced cheeses
6 oz. marinated artichoke hearts, drained
2 1/4 oz. sliced black olives, drained
2 to 3 lg. dill pickles, sliced lengthwise
1 mild red or white onion, sliced

OPTIONAL:
Mayonnaise
2 oz. anchovy fillets, drained

Cut bread in half horizontally. Hollow out the soft bread from top and bottom, leaving 1/2 to 3/4 inch shell. In small bowl combine the olive oil with the garlic. Brush cut surfaces of bread shells with oil. Spread with mayonnaise if desired.

To assemble: Layer 1/3 of tomato slices on the bottom bread crust, then top with alternate layers of meats, pepperoni, cheeses, 1/2 the remaining tomatoes, artichoke hearts, olives, pickles, onion and anchovies, if desired. Top with remaining tomatoes and place the top crust on the filling, pressing down firmly. Seal the sandwich tightly in plastic wrap and foil.

If made ahead, refrigerate. Just before serving, place the wrapped sandwich on a flat surface and press down firmly on top to flatten it. Unwrap and cut into wedges.

CHAMPION CHEESE STEAK SANDWICH

1/2 lb. Velveeta, cubed
1/2 c. Mayonnaise
1/4 c. milk
1 tsp. dry mustard
1 med. onion, sliced
2 tbsp. Margarine or butter
1 lb. thin roast beef slices
6"-8" French bread rolls, split

Combine process cheese spread, mayo, milk and mustard. Stir over low heat until smooth. Sauté onions in margarine. Add meat; mix lightly until thoroughly heated. Fill rolls with meat mixture. Top with sauce.

CHARLIE'S WRAP SANDWICH

2	Tbsp	Extra Virgin Olive Oil
		Sautéed Peppers
1	Bunch	Arugula Lettuce or Any Other Variety
1	Tbsp	Chopped Sun Dried Tomatoes
2	Tbsp	Goat Cheese
1	Tbsp	Sherry Vinegar
1/2		green pepper
1/2		yellow red pepper
2	Large	sweet red pepper
1	Tbsp	Extra Virgin Olive Oil

1. Heat 1 table spoon of extra virgin olive oil in a hot skillet. Add 2 large sweet red peppers. 1/2 yellow pepper, 1/2 green pepper - seeded, cored, cut into strips and sauté, until soft.

2. Remove from the heat and sprinkle with half of the sherry vinegar.

3. Spread 2 tablespoons of goat cheese on the flour tortillas, or wraps. Scatter 1 tablespoon of chopped sun dried tomatoes on the wrap. Divide the sautéed peppers on top of tortilla, making sure they are in the center of the tortilla.

4. Toss 1 bunch of arugula lettuce (or any other variety of lettuce that you choose) with 2 tablespoons of extra virgin olive oil and the rest of the sherry vinegar. Place tossed arugula in the center of tortilla.

5. Fold about of inch of the tortilla from top and bottom over the filling. Turn the wrap sideways and roll it up. Wrap in wax paper or tin foil.

6. Serve at room temperature.

CHEDDAR APPLE SMOKED TURKEY SANDWICH

1/4	Cup	Hellmann's Dijonnaise Creamy Mustard Blend
2	Tbsp	Honey
8	Slices	Seven-Grain or Whole Wheat Bread
4	Ounces	sliced or 1 cup shredded cheddar cheese
1/2	Pound	sliced Smoked turkey or ham
1		Apple, cored and thinly sliced

1. In small bowl combine creamy mustard blend and honey; spread on one side of each slice of bread.

2. Layer cheese on 4 bread slices; top with turkey, apple and remaining bread. Cut sandwiches in half.

CHEF SALAD SANDWICH

4 slices fresh dark rye bread
2 tsp. butter
Iceberg or leaf lettuce
1/2 c. Thousand Island dressing
1 (3 oz.) pkgs. water-sliced cooked ham
1 (3 oz.) pkg. water-sliced smoked turkey
4 oz. sliced Swiss cheese
2 hard cooked eggs
8 black olives, pitted
8 red cherry tomatoes
4 sweet gherkins
6 slices crisp, cooked bacon
4 slices dark rye bread, toasted, buttered

1. Butter the untoasted bread. Place it on each of four serving plates.

2. Top each slice with lettuce.

3. Spread 2 tablespoons of dressing over lettuce.

4. Divide the ham and turkey into four portions each. Arrange on top of each serving. Top with cheese, cut into julienne sticks.

5. Arrange on each sandwich 2 quarters of hard cooked eggs, 2 black olives, 2 red cherry tomatoes, halved, and 1 sweet gherkin, halved.

6. Top with bacon. Add more dressing or pass dressing in a small bowl.

7. Surround with toasted rye bread, cut into quarters. 4 servings.

CHICAGO ITALIAN BEEF SANDWICHES

    2 lb leftover beef roast
       Roasting pan drippings
    2 tbsp fresh oregano, finely chopped
       OR 2 teaspoon dried oregano, crushed
    1 tbsp fresh sweet basil, finely chopped
       OR 1 teaspoon dried basil, crushed
    1 tsp whole black peppercorns
  1/2 tsp red pepper, ground (1/2 to 1)
    1 tbsp fresh parsley, minced
       Salt, to taste
    3 cloves garlic, minced
    1   fresh green pepper seeded, sliced into 1/4 inch strips

Thinly slice cooked, roast beef and place in a Dutch oven (or put it back into the same pan in which the beef was roasted). Add enough water to cover. Add remaining ingredients and bring to simmer.

After the beef has cooked for awhile, taste and adjust seasonings. Cook about 1 hour. Serve beef on Italian bread with grilled green peppers and/or giardiniera relish.

Serve the gravy as a dip.

CHICKADO'WICHES

2 (1 oz.) slices Italian bread
1 tbsp. Thousand Island dressing, divided
2 oz. thinly sliced cooked chicken
2 slices crisp bacon, crumbled
1/4 c. green onions
1/4 c. tomatoes
1/8 med. avocado (1 oz.), pared and thinly sliced
2 oz. Swiss cheese, sliced

Toast the Italian bread to taste and arrange slices in a single layer on a baking sheet. Spread each slice of bread with 1/2 teaspoon Thousand Island dressing. Top each slice with half of the chicken, bacon, onions, and tomato, then top each with 1 teaspoon of the remaining dressing. Arrange half of the avocado slices and half of the cheese on each sandwich. Broil 6 inches from heat source until sandwich is hot and cheese is melted, about 2 minutes. Makes 2 servings.

CHICKEN AND PEPPERS SANDWICHES

4 boneless, skinless chicken breast halves (1lb.)
2 tbsp. lemon juice
2 tbsp. water
2 tbsp. olive oil
1 tsp. dried whole basil
1 tsp. dried whole oregano
1 clove garlic, crushed
Dash of pepper
Vegetable cooking spray
1/2 c. (2 oz.) shredded part skim Mozzarella cheese
3 tbsp. finely chopped green pepper
3 tbsp. finely chopped sweet red pepper
2 tbsp. finely chopped onion
4 curly leaf lettuce leaves
2 whole wheat hamburger buns, split

Trim excess fat from chicken breast halves. Place chicken between 2 sheets of wax paper, and flatten to 1/4 inch thickness, using a meat mallet or rolling pin. Place chicken breast halves in a shallow container. Combine lemon juice and next 6 ingredients, stirring well. Pour over chicken. Cover and marinate in refrigerator 2 hours. Remove chicken from marinade, reserving marinade. Arrange chicken on a grill coated with cooking spray. Grill 6 inches over hot coals 15 minutes, turning and basting with reserved marinade every 5 minutes. Remove chicken from grill, and sprinkle with cheese. Set chicken aside, and keep warm. Coat a medium skillet with cooking spray. Place over medium heat until hot. Add green pepper, sweet red pepper, and onion. Saute 2 minutes or until tender. Remove from heat. Place lettuce leaves on 4 bun halves. Place reserved chicken on lettuce leaves. Top each bun half with 2 tablespoon pepper mixture. Yield: 4 servings

CHICKEN CLUB SANDWICH

Boneless, skinless chicken breasts
Mayonnaise
Dijon mustard
Seasoned bread crumbs
Thin sliced ham
Swiss cheese
Toothpicks

Brush one side of each chicken breast with mayonnaise. Brush the other side of each chicken breast with mustard. Cover both sides well with seasoned bread crumbs.
Place a slice of ham and a slice of cheese on one side of the coated breast. Roll the breast, with cheese and ham inside, into a tight package and secure with a toothpick.

Bake at 350 degrees until done.

CHICKEN SANDWICHES

1 lg. or 2 sm. chickens
3 eggs
Salt and pepper
Celery salt
2 to 3 slices dry bread
Chicken broth

Cook chicken and remove meat from bones. Shred chicken; do not grind. Add beaten eggs, salt, pepper, celery salt and broken up bread. Add chicken broth to make right consistency for a sandwich. Bake at 350 degrees for 1 hour or longer, if needed.

CHICKEN SLOPPY JOE

1 tbsp vegetable oil
1 lb ground chicken
1   green bell pepper; chopped
1 med onion; chopped
30 oz canned sloppy joe sauce
3 cups cooked rice
6   hamburger buns or- English muffins

Heat oil in a large skillet over medium-high heat until hot. Add chicken; cook and stir 4 to 6 minutes or until no longer pink. Stir in pepper and onion; cook 1 to 3 minutes. Add sloppy joe sauce.

Cookover medium heat about 8 to 10 minutes; stirring occasionally.

Stir in rice; cook until thoroughly heated. Spoon over hamburger buns.

CIRCULAR SANDWICH

```
1      red bell pepper
1      yellow bell pepper
1      medium eggplant
Olive oil
salt and freshly ground  pepper
1         10 inch round loaf crusty bread
1/2 c    oregano lemon dressing
1/4 lb   slice black forest ham
1/2 lb   salami, preferably 2 kinds
1 lb     mozzarella, sliced
20        large fresh basil leaves
```

Roast whole peppers over a gas flame or under a broiler until they are completely blackened. Place in a paper bag until cool enough to handle.

Peel, cut in half and seed. Cut eggplant into 1/2 inch slices. Brush with olive oil and sear on a grill or hot skillet until brown on both sides.

Season with salt and pepper. Cut bread in half horizontally with a serrated knife, and hollow out the top and bottom halves. Brush bottom half with 1/4 cup of the dressing. In the bottom half of the bread, place the fillings in this order: ham, eggplant, one kind of salami, peppers, mozzarella, remaining salami and basil. Brush inside of top half with remaining dressing. Place top half onto sandwich.

Wrap sandwich tightly in waxed paper or plastic wrap.

Place a tray or baking sheet on top of the sandwich and weight it with several cans for about 1 hour.

COLD TURKEY REUBEN SANDWICH

4	tsp	Plain Low-fat yogurt
8	slices	Rye Bread
8	oz	Cooked turkey breast thinly sliced
1-1/3	c	Sweet & Sour Red Cabbage-drained (recipe to follow)

-----SWEET & SOUR RED CABBAGE-----

1	lb	Red cabbage -- shredded
1/2	c	Cider vinegar
1/2	c	Water
2	tbsp	Margarine
1/2	tsp	Salt
2 tbsp		Sugar or to taste

SANDWICH: Spread 1 teaspoon yogurt on each 4 slices of rye bread.

Place the sliced turkey on the 4 bread slices. Spoon 1/3 of the Sweet and Sour Red Cabbage on each sandwich; top with remaining bread.

SWEET AND SOUR RED CABBAGE: Put cabbage, vinegar, water, margarine, and salt in a deep cooking pot. Cover and cook about 15 minutes or until crisp-tender, lifting and turning with a large kitchen fork two or three times.   Remove from heat. Add sweetener to cabbage gradually, lifting and mixing well with a fork. Drain off any liquid.

CRISPY FRIED FISH SANDWICHES

1 lb. fresh or frozen fish fillets (haddock, cod, or halibut)
1 egg, slightly beaten
1 c. crumbs (cracker, dried bread or corn flakes)
Crisco oil for frying
6 buns
6 sandwich buns
6 tbsp. tartar sauce

Cut fresh or partially thawed fish into 6 (3 inch) squares about 1/2 inch thick. Dip fish portions in egg, then in crumbs. Fry fish in 1/4 to 1/2 inch Crisco oil heated to 350 degrees in electric skillet until golden brown, about 4-6 minutes on each side. Drain on paper toweling. Place one slice of cheese on bottom half of sandwich bun. Top with hot fried fish. Spread 1 tablespoon tartar sauce over fish. Cover with top half of bun.

CRUNCHY TURKEY MELT SANDWICHES

2	Cups	chopped cooked turkey
1/2	Cup	KRAFT Natural Shredded Cheddar Cheese
1/3	Cup	KRAFT Mayo Light Mayonnaise
2	Tablespoons	finely chopped onion
2	Teaspoons	KRAFT Pure Prepared Mustard
1/4	Teaspoon	pepper
8		Claussen Sandwich Slices -- up to 12
4		sandwich or hamburger buns

MIX turkey, cheese, mayo, onion, mustard and pepper.

ARRANGE 2 to 3 pickle slices on bottom half of each bun. Top each with 1/2
cup turkey mixture and top halves of buns. Place sandwiches on cookie
sheet; cover tightly with foil.

BAKE at 350°F for 15 minutes.

CROQUE-MONSIEUR HAM & CHEESE SANDWICH

1 c. (4 oz.) grated Swiss cheese
1/4 c. light cream
8 slices bread
8 slices boiled ham
2 eggs, slightly beaten
1/4 c. milk
1/2 tsp. salt
Cheese Sauce*

Combine Swiss cheese and cream to make a paste; spread on each slice of bread. Place a slice of ham on each slice of bread; close to form a sandwich. Beat together eggs, milk and salt in a shallow dish; dip bread on both sides in egg/milk mixture. Fry on lightly buttered griddle or in skillet until brown on both sides and cheese has melted. Serve alone or with cheese sauce.
Serves 4.

*CHEESE SAUCE:
1 tbsp. butter
1 tbsp. flour
1/2 tsp. dry mustard
1 c. milk
1 c. (4 oz.) shredded Cheddar cheese
Cherry tomatoes (optional garnish)
Green pepper (optional garnish)

Melt butter in 1 quart saucepan; blend in flour and mustard, cook, stirring until smooth. Slowly stir in milk stirring constantly until thick. Remove from heat, stir in cheese until melted. Garnish with sliced cherry tomato and green pepper, if desired.

DAGWOOD BUMSTEAD SANDWICH

3	lg	Onions
1		Head lettuce
4		Tomatoes, sliced
1		Lobster tail
1		Eagle talon
1		Fish (pref.2-days old)
1		Pot spaghetti
		- Cold and gooey
1	lb	Bacon (cooked)
1		Meatloaf
1		Ham
1		Fried egg (over easy)
1		String of sausages
1		Mayonnaise, gallon
1		Jar of pickle relish
1		Tin of sardine in oil
1		Bottle of ketchup
1		Bottle Sweet mustard
1		Hot mustard
1		Loaf Bread
		Assorted cheese
		Assorted vegetables
		Assorted olives

DIRECTIONS: Arrange the ingredients between two slices of bread. Serves one.

DAGWOOD ITALIANO

1		Bell pepper, red
1		Bell pepper, green
1-1/2	tsp	Olive oil, divided
1	tsp	Rosemary, fresh chopped
		Or
1/4	tsp	Dried crushed
1		Garlic, clove, minced
1	tbsp	Red wine or broth
12	oz	Lamb, boneless loin, sirloin
4		French bread 5"length
1/2	c	Mozzarella, low fat, grated
1/4	c	Parmesan cheese

Roast red and green bell peppers in preheated 400*F oven 20-25 minutes, or until skins are slightly charred and shriveled. Remove from oven, transfer to plate, wrap with plastic wrap and let stand 10 minutes.

Remove peppers from plastic, peel off skin remove seeds and cut into strips. Set aside. In large bowl combine rosemary, 1/2 teaspoon of the olive oil, garlic and wine or broth; add lamb and marinate 1 hour. Heat remaining oil in a large nonstick skillet. Add lamb and sear on all sides.

Place lamb on rack in shallow roasting pan. Insert a meat thermometer in center part of lamb and roast in preheated 375*F. oven to internal temp of 140*F. about 27-34 minutes, or to desired doneness. Or grill 15-20 minutes.

To construct sandwiches thinly slice lamb and arrange on four of the bread halves, alternating with red and green pepper strips. Top with mozzarella and Parmesan cheese. Pace under broiler until cheeses melt, bubble and turn light brown. Add top halves of bread and serve.

DELUXE CHICKEN SANDWICH

1 (6 oz.) can Swanson premium chunk white chicken, drained
1/3 c. chopped cucumber
1 tbsp. non-fat mayonnaise dressing
1/8 tsp. dried dill weed, crushed
2 sandwich buns, split
Spinach leaves
Tomato slices

In medium bowl combine chicken, chopped cucumber, mayo, dressing
and dill weed; toss gently to mix well.
Cover; refrigerate for 2 to 4 hours. Serve on bottom halves of
sandwich buns, arrange spinach, tomato
and chicken filling. Replace top halves.

Makes 2 sandwiches.

DIJON CHEESESTEAK SANDWICHES

1/2 lb. Velveeta cheese, cubed
1/4 c. milk
1 tbsp. Dijon mustard
1/4 c. green onion slices
2 tbsp. margarine
1 lb. thin roast beef slices
6 (8 inch) French bread rolls, split

Combine Velveeta cheese, milk and mustard in saucepan; stir over low heat until smooth.
Saute onions in margarine. Add meat, mix lightly until thoroughly heated.
Fill rolls with meat mixture - top with sauce. Makes 6 sandwiches.

DOUBLE-DECKER CHEESE MELT

1	c	shredded cheddar cheese
1/4	c	butter or margarine -- softened
1		egg
1/2	tsp	garlic salt
1/2	tsp	onion salt
6	slices	white bread
		paprika -- optional

In a food processor, blend cheese and butter. Add the egg, garlic salt and onion salt; process for 1 minutes or until creamy. Spread 2 tbsp on each slice of bread. Stack two slices of bread, cheese side up, for each sandwich; sprinkle with paprika if desired.   Cut each sandwich in half diagonally.   Place on an ungreased baking sheet. Bake at 400 for 12-15 minutes or until golden and bubbly.

EASY PIZZA BURGERS

1 (12 oz.) can Spam, ground
1 lg. can Hormel Chili Without Beans
2 c. American cheese, shredded
1/2 c. onion, chopped

Mix all ingredients together. Spread on open-faced hamburger bun. Place on cookie sheet and broil in oven for 5 minutes or until cheese is melted and edges are brown.

EGG SALAD SANDWICH

1 tbsp. butter
2 tbsp. sugar
3 tsp. vinegar
1/2 c. milk
1 tbsp. flour
1 egg, beaten

Combine all ingredients, stirring constantly. Boil until thick.
Remove from heat and add:
9 eggs, hard-boiled, 8 oz. cream cheese, 2 tbsp. onion, minced, 1 sm. can pimento, finely cut.

Stir and refrigerate until all is cold.

EVERYONES FAVORITE PASTRAMI SANDWICH

      6 oz sliced pastrami
      2 TB whole-grain mustard
      4 oz beer
      3 slices of onion rings intact
      1 TB oil
:   Salt and pepper
      2 slices rye bread or thick crusty brown bread

Preheat a grill. Season onions with salt and pepper and brush with oil. In a small saucepan combine beer and mustard and bring to a boil. Add pastrami and simmer for 3 minutes. Grill onions on both sides and toast bread on a cooler part of the grill. When all ingredients are heated, prepare sandwich.

FAST SKILLET BEEF KABOB SANDWICH

1 lb.   well-trimmed boneless beef top sirloin steak, 1 inch thick, cut
into 1-1/2" cubes

1 tsp. each garlic powder, lemon-pepper and char-grill seasonings
2 tbsp. butter (divided)
1 med. onion (sliced thin)
1 each lg. green and red peppers (cut into rings)
2 (6 inch) pita bread rounds (cut into halves)
Tomato wedges
Parsley sprigs

Place steak cubes in a small bowl; sprinkle with garlic powder and
lemon-pepper seasoning. Set aside.
Over medium-high heat, sprinkle char-grill seasoning into a large iron
skillet. Add one tablespoon butter, melt and add beef cubes. Cook 5 to
7 minutes, turning once. Remove beef cubes to heated platter to keep
warm.
Add reserved butter to same skillet and melt. Add onion and pepper
rings. Stir fry 3 minutes.
To serve, arrange pepper rings on platter, alternating colors. Spoon
beef cubes inside and outside of rings.

FIESTA STYLE SLOPPY JOE

1	Pkg	Refrigerated Flaky Biscuits
1	Pound	ground beef
1	Small	onion -- chopped
1	11 oz	can mexicorn
1	Can	condensed tomato soup
1/4	Cup	water
1-1/4	Tsp	chili powder
1/8	Tsp	hot pepper sauce -- up to 1/4

Heat oven to 375 F. Bake biscuits or as directed on can. Meanwhile, in large skillet brown ground beef, bell pepper and onion. Drain. Stir in remaining ingredients. Bring to a boil. Reduce heat; cover and simmer 10 minutes or until thoroughly heated.

To serve, split warm biscuits; place 2 halves on each plate. Spoon hot beef mixture over biscuit halves.

FRENCH TOAST CHEDDAR SANDWICHES

2	large eggs
1/3 c	Milk or Light Cream
1/2 tsp	Salt
8	White Bread; Slices
	Prepared mustard of choice
4	Thick Slices Cheddar Cheese
3 tbsp	Butter

Set out a heavy skillet or cast iron griddle. Beat the eggs slightly in a shallow bowl and add the milk or cream and salt, set aside.

Spread the bread slices out on a flat working surface. Spread one side of four slices of bread lightly with the prepared mustard. Top each with a slice of cheddar cheese. Butter the remaining four slices of bread and top each cheese slice with bread, butter side down. Heat the butter in the skillet or on the griddle. Carefully dip each sandwich into the egg mixture, coating both sides. Allow the excess egg mixture to drain back into the bowl. Dip only as many sandwiches as will lie flat in the skillet or griddle. Cook over low heat until browned. Turn and brown the other sides. Repeat for the remaining sandwiches and if necessary, add more butter to the skillet or griddle to prevent sticking.

Instead of grilling, you can place the sandwiches, after dipping, on a well greased baking sheet and brown in the oven at 450 degrees F. for 8 to 10 minutes. Serve hot.

FRENCH TOASTED SANDWICHES

3 eggs, beaten
1/2 c. milk
1 tsp. sugar
1/4 tsp. salt
Ham, chicken, turkey, corn beef, or cheese slices
1/4 c. melted butter or margarine
12 slices bread

Using your favorite bread and 1 of the fillings, make up to 6
sandwiches.
Beat together eggs, milk, sugar, and salt in pie plate with fork. Dip
each mixture, turning to coat both sides.

Brown sandwiches on both sides in melted butter or margarine in
medium skillet over medium high heat.

GERMAN BEEFSTEAKS

1	Hard roll; large, dry
1/2 c	Water
4 tbsp	vegetable oil
1	medium onion, chopped
1 lb	ground beef; lean
1/2 tsp	Salt
1/4 tsp	Pepper
4	medium onions, sliced for garnish

In a small bowl soak roll in water. Heat 2 tbsp vegetable oil in a frying pan; cook chopped onion until lightly browned. Transfer onion to a bowl.

Squeeze roll as dry as possible and mix roll with onion. Add ground beef; blend well. Season with salt and pepper. Shape meat into 4 patties; cook about 5 minutes on each side or to desired doneness. Remove and keep warm.

Add sliced onions to pan drippings; cook until lightly browned. Arrange beefsteaks on a platter and top with onion rings.

GLORIFIED BLT

1 piece toasted bread
Lettuce, shredded
Onion, thinly sliced
Tomato, thinly sliced
Cover this with cheese sauce, topped with two or three pieces of crisp bacon.

--CHEESE SAUCE:--
2 tbsp. butter, melted
2 tbsp. flour
Salt and pepper

Add one cup of milk. When thickened, add 1 cup grated cheese. Cook until thick, stirring all the time.

GRANDMA'S TUNA-CHEESE SANDWICHES

1 lb. Velveeta cheese, diced
2 (7 oz.) cans tuna
1/2 c. chopped olives
1 (10 oz.) can tomato puree
2 tbsp. onion, minced
2 tbsp. green pepper, chopped
2 tbsp. celery, diced

Mix and let stand several hours in refrigerator. Spread generously on hamburger buns (16).
Wrap in foil and bake 45 minutes at 250 degrees.

GREEK GYROS

Prepare Cucumber Yogurt Sauce (recipe below) cover and refrigerate

1 pound lean ground lamb
2 cloves garlic
1 1/2 teaspoons dried oregano leaves, crushed
1 teaspoon onion powder
1 teaspoon salt
3/4 teaspoon pepper
1 large tomato, cut in half and then into slices
1 small onion, thinly sliced
4 whole pita pocket breads, cut in half, warmed

In a large bowl, combine lamb, garlic, dried oregano leaves, onion powder, salt and pepper; mix lightly but thoroughly. Shape into two oval 1/2-inch thick patties.

Place patties on rack in broiler pan so surface of meat is 3 to 4 inches from heat. Broil 8 to 10 minutes or until no longer pink, turning once. Carve each patty into thin slices. Place equal amounts of lamb, tomato and onion in each pita half; serve with Cucumber Yogurt Sauce. Serves 4.

Cucumber Yogurt Sauce

8-ounce carton plain low-fat yogurt
1/3 cup seeded, chopped cucumber
2 tablespoons finely chopped onion
1 clove garlic, crushed
1 teaspoon sugar

In medium bowl, combine all ingredients; mix well. Serve with Lamb Gyros.

42

GRILLED CHEESE-CHIPOTLE SANDWICH

4	slices	White or wheat bread
2	tsp	Pureed chipotle chiles
5	oz	Cheese - shredded or thinly sliced
1		Ripe tomato -- sliced
		Thinly sliced red onion
		Cilantro leaves- coarsely chopped
		Soft butter

SPREAD EACH PIECE OF BREAD with thin coating of pureed chiles, or more if you like your sandwich really hot.

Cover the bottom slice with layer of cheese, tomato and onion slices and as much cilantro as you like. Top with second slice of bread and butter it. Place sandwich, butter-side down, in cast-iron skillet. Spread top piece of bread with butter as well and cook sandwich slowly. When golden brown on bottom, turn it over and cook on the other side. Covering pan will help melt cheese by the time bread is crisped and golden.

GRILLED CUBAN SANDWICH

8	slices	pork loin -- 1 ounce each
8	slices	ham, -- 1 ounce each
12	dill	pickle chips
8	slices	Swiss cheese
4		sandwich rolls
		Dijon mustard to taste

Prepare a wood or charcoal fire and allow it to burn to embers. Layer each sandwich with the cheese, ham, pork, and pickles.

Grill the sandwich, top side down for 1 minute, turn over and place a sauté pan on top and continue to cook until cheese is melted about 3 to 4 minutes.

GRILLED PORTABELLO MUSHROOM SANDWICH

Marinade:

2	tablespoons	rice wine vinegar
2	tablespoons	lemon juice
2	tablespoons	olive oil
1	clove	garlic -- minced
2	teaspoons	dried oregano
1	Pinch	kosher salt
1	Pinch	sugar
1	Pinch	black pepper -- freshly ground

RECIPE

2	large	Portobello mushrooms
1	large clove	garlic
2	tablespoons	mayonnaise
2	teaspoons	fresh thyme -- chopped
1	red bell pepper -- roasted	
2	teaspoons	balsamic vinegar
2	onion rolls -- split & grilled	
2	teaspoons	balsamic vinegar
2	thick slices	Monterey jack cheese

Combine marinade ingredients. Marinate mushroom in this mixture 1-2 hours.

Mash other garlic clove into fine paste. Stir into mayonnaise and add thyme.

On barbecue grill or under broiler, cook mushrooms 5 minutes on each side, or until soft. Sprinkle red bell pepper with balsamic vinegar and shallots. Grill or lightly toast onion rolls. Spread mayonnaise on each half of rolls. Place grilled mushrooms on two onion roll halves, cover with roasted bell pepper, cheese and top half of rolls. Cut in half and serve hot.

GRILLED SALMON & CHEDDAR SANDWICHES

1 lb can	Salmon
1 tsp	Onion -- grated
10 oz	medium Cheddar*
1 tsp	Lemon juice
1/4 c	Mayonnaise

* Slice the Cheddar Cheese into 4 slices of 2 1/2 ozs each.

Mix the salmon with the onion, lemon juice, and mayonnaise. Spread the mixture on thick slices of French bread and top with a slice of cheddar cheese. Add a top slice of bread and butter both sides of the sandwich generously. Grill until brown, then turn and brown the other side, and the cheese is melted. Serve hot.

GRILLED TUNA AND DILL HAVARTI SANDWICH

If you can't find semolina bread (crusty Italian bread made with semolina flour), use an Italian or sandwich loaf.

1 (6 1/2 or 7 oz.) can solid white tuna, drained & flaked
3 tbsp. mayonnaise
2 tbsp. celery, diced
1 tbsp. parsley, chopped
1 tbsp. red onion, diced
1/4 tsp. freshly ground pepper
1 loaf (about 14 inches) semolina bread
1 c. shredded dill Havarti cheese
4 tbsp. butter or margarine, softened

In small bowl, combine tuna, mayonnaise, celery, parsley, onion and pepper until well blended.
Cut bread on a sharp diagonal into eight 1/2 inch slices, each about 6 inches long.
(Reserve any remaining bread for another use.) Layer each of 4 slices with 1/4 cup tuna mixture and 1/4 cup grated cheese.
Spread each remaining slice lightly with about 1/2 tablespoon butter and place buttered side up on cheese.
In large heavy skillet, cook sandwiches buttered side down over high heat until golden. Butter tops lightly; turn with a large spatula and cook other sides until golden. Makes 4 sandwiches,

GOLDEN WEST SANDWICH

2 slices bread
2 slices American cheese
1 slice boiled ham

Make sandwich, ham between the cheese. Then dip in batter of 1 egg beaten, plus 4 tablespoon milk
.
Brown in greased frying pan. (A nice luncheon dish.)

HALF-TIME BEEF SANDWICHES

2	tsp	Lemon juice
1		Small apple, finely chopped
1		3-oz pkg. cream cheese
1	tbsp	Milk
1	tbsp	Prepared horseradish
1/4	c	Walnut pieces
6	ea	Kaiser rolls, split
6	ea	Lettuce leaves
1	lb	thinly sliced roast beef
2	tbsp	Sliced green onions

Sprinkle lemon juice over apple. Combine cream cheese, milk and horseradish. Stir in apple and walnut pieces. Spread cut sides of rolls with equal amounts of the cream cheese mixture.

Place equal amounts of lettuce, beef and green onion on each bottom roll half. Cover with tops.

HAM AND SWISS SANDWICHES

1/2 c. melted butter
2 tbsp. grated onion
1 tbsp. poppy seed
2 tbsp. mustard
2 tbsp. mayonnaise
Ham, sliced very thin
Swiss cheese, sliced very thin
Bi-Lo Dinner rolls, or Tatum rolls

Mix together first five ingredients. Cool and stir to distribute poppy seeds throughout.
Refrigerate at least 2 hours. Split rolls and spread generous amount of dressing on each side.
Pile the ham and cheese on the rolls, close and serve.

HAWAIIAN CRESCENT SANDWICHES

1 can Pillsbury quick crescent dinner rolls
1 can sm. chunk style ham (Hormel)
1/3 c. crushed pineapple, drained
1/2 c. shredded Monterey Jack cheese
1/4 c. diced green pepper

Press dough into 4 rectangles (7x4 inches). Place dough on ungreased cookie sheet.
Press perforations to seal. In a bowl mix ham, pineapple, cheese and green pepper.
Evenly divide mixture into rectangle; fold over to cover. Bake 13-18 minutes or until golden.
Serve with fruit salad or tossed salad or a cup of soup.

HAWAIIAN FARMER SANDWICHES

12 slices bread
Softened butter
1 1/3 c. diced cooked chicken
1 1/2 c. diced cooked ham
1/2 c. crushed pineapple, well drained
1/3 c. mayonnaise
3 tbsp. finely chopped pecans (I use 1/4 c. rounded)
1 1/2 tbsp. chopped green pepper (opt.)
1 tsp. thinly sliced green onion (opt.)
1/4 tsp. salt (if ham is salty, this is not needed)
Dash of black pepper
6 slices Mozzarella cheese

Butter one side of bread, mix ingredients except cheese, divide mixture equally on unbuttered side of (6) slices of bread and top each with slice of cheese. Close sandwiches with the remaining bread buttered side out.
Grill on both sides until cheese starts to melt and sandwiches are golden.
(Use canned chunk chicken and chunk ham, drained and omit the salt for convenience)

HERO SANDWICH

3/4 lb. ground beef
1/3 c. evaporated milk
1/4 c. ground cracker crumbs (bread)
1 egg
1/4 c. chopped onion
1 tsp. prepared mustard
1/8 tsp. pepper
3/4 tsp. salt
1 c. grated cheese

Mix together and bake at 350 degrees for 40 minutes. Wrap in foil and spread on buns or bread as needed.

HIGH ROLLER SANDWICHES

1   Bag flour tortillas
8 oz softened cream cheese
   Roast beef sliced thin
   Ham sliced thin
   Turkey sliced thin
   Colby Jack cheese sliced thin
   Lettuce shredded thin strips
   Garlic powder
   Sliced tomatoes very thin

Use the back of a spatula and cover each tortilla with a thin layer of cream cheese. Sprinkle lightly with garlic powder.

Layer meats, cheese, lettuce, and tomatoes on half of each tortilla. Then roll up tortilla starting at the filled end with cream cheese side rolled up last so it will seal.

Cut in 1 inch pieces and serve. Serve 8-10

HOE DOWN SANDWICHES

4 hard-cooked eggs, chopped
3/4 c. ham, chopped
16 whole wheat bread slices
16 cheese slices
1/4 c. celery, chopped
1/4 c. dill pickle, chopped
Salad dressing
Margarine

Combine eggs, ham, celery, pickle and enough salad dressing to
moisten. Mix lightly.
For each sandwich, cover slice of bread with cheese, egg mixture and
second slice of cheese and second slice of bread.
Spread bread with margarine. Place sandwich on cookie sheet. Broil on
each side until golden brown and cheese melts.
Makes 8 sandwiches.

HOT ITALIAN MEATBALL SANDWICHES

1	lb	good quality ground beef
1/2	lb	ground pork
1/2	cup	cornflake crumbs
1/4	cup	evaporated milk
1		egg
2	tbsp	dried onion flakes
1	8 oz block	mozzarella cheese
1	tsp	Italian seasoning
2	cups	your favorite pizza sauce
6	slices	mozzarella cheese
6		submarine sandwich rolls

Combine beef, pork, crumbs, milk, egg, Italian seasoning, and onion. Mix well and form into 1 1/2 inch meatballs. Cube the mozzarella into 1/2" cubes.   Press 1 cube into each meatball, cover well with the meat. Place on ungreased cookie sheet and bake for 18-20 minutes. In a saucepan heat the pizza sauce. Add meatballs and warm through.

Slice a V shaped lengthwise cut into sub rolls.
Use the cut out for breadcrumbs later. Pile down the cut 5-6 meatballs. Spoon on sauce and lay a slice of mozzarella cut in half so it covers the length of the roll on the top of the sandwich. Place under the broiler for 2-3 minutes or until bubbly.

HOT SALAD SANDWICHES

1 c. shredded cheddar cheese
1/2 c. diced cucumber
1 tbsp. minced onion
1/4 c. sour cream
1/8 tsp. chili powder
4 slices bread, toasted
4 lg. thick tomato slices
8 slices dill pickle
Paprika

Mix cheese, cucumber, onion, sour cream and chili powder. Arrange 1 tomato slice and 2 pickle slices on each bread slice. Divide cheese mixture over the 4 slices.

Sprinkle with paprika. Broil until cheese melts and is heated through.

HULA HAM SANDWICH

1	can	(20-oz) Dole pineapple slices
5		Kaiser rolls, cut in half
4	teas	Dijon mustard, spread over bottom of roll -halves
1		lettuce leaf
2	slices	Swiss cheese
4	ounces	deli-sliced smoked ham
2		pineapple slices

Drain pineapple slices, slice rolls in half. Spread Dijon mustard over bottom of rolls. Layer on each bottom; lettuce, cheese, ham and pineapple.

INTERNATIONAL TURKEY SANDWICH

1	cup	finely shredded lettuce
1	cup	finely diced tomato
3		finely chopped scallions
1/2	cup	finely chopped green pepper
2	tbsp	Italian dressing
2		halved English muffins
8	ounces	sliced -- cooked turkey
4	ounces	sliced Monterey Jack cheese

Combine lettuce, tomato, scallions and green pepper in a large bowl. Pour on Italian dressing and toss well.

Arrange 2 ounces turkey and 1 ounce cheese on each muffin half. For a warm sandwich broil 2-3 minutes before spooning 1/4 of the salad on each open face sandwich.

ITALIAN ROAST BEEF SANDWICH

4-6 lbs. roast beef
3-4 lg. onions
1 tbsp. salt
1/4 tsp. pepper
1/2 tsp. marjoram
1-2 lg. carrots
1/2 tsp. salt
1/2 tsp. garlic
1/2 tsp. Italian seasoning
1/2 tsp. seasoning salt
1/4 tsp. basil
1/2 tsp. oregano

Place beef in roasting pan. Fill pan half full with water. Sprinkle roast with half of the tablespoon salt,
put remainder in water. Lay sliced onion and carrots over roast and in water. Sprinkle with marjoram.
Roast meat at 350 degree in covered pan 3-4 hours. Refrigerate roast overnight in broth.
Next day, slice very thin. Bring beef broth to boil, add seasonings and simmer 5 minutes.
Carefully lay sliced beef into broth, keeping slices intact. Pour broth over beef. Cover and heat in 350 degree oven.
Serve on buttered buns or hard rolls. (Butter keeps rolls from getting soggy.) Serves 12-14.

ITALIAN SUBMARINE SANDWICH

8 slices hard salami
4 slices Mortadella or bologna
4 slices summer sausage
4 slices ham (meats can be substituted)
1 sm. zucchini squash
1/2 c. Italian style dressing or
French bread or Italian bread
1/4 c. butter or margarine
1/4 tsp. oregano
1/4 tsp. basil
Lettuce
3 slices Mozzarella cheese cut in half diagonally
6 to 8 onion rings
4 green pepper rings
4 tomato slices
4 stuffed olives, sliced

Cut zucchini squash in thin slices and marinate in Italian dressing while preparing sandwich.
Slice loaf of bread in half lengthwise, separating top and bottom of loaf. Blend butter with oregano
and basil and spread on cut surfaces of bread. Cover bottom half with lettuce. Arrange half slices of cheese and onion rings on lettuce.
Alternate folded slices of meat on top, overlapping partially. Arrange green pepper rings and tomato slices over meat.
Drain zucchini and overlap slices over tomatoes. Garnish with stuffed olives. Cover with buttered top of loaf. Slice and serve.

JOEGIE

9 inch white or wheat italian sub roll or hoagie roll

1-1/2	ounces	capicola
1-1/2	ounces	genoa salami -- sliced
1-1/2	ounces	provolone cheese -- sliced
		shredded lettuce
		sliced tomatoes
		hot peppers (opt.)
		italian dressing

Slice open sub roll lengthwise. Drizzle Italian dressing on the bread.
Layer roll with meat then cheese slices then top with lettuce, tomatoes
and hot peppers.

Sprinkle with dressing if desired.

LIBERTY BELL STEAK SANDWICH

1 lg. onion, sliced
2 tbsp. margarine
1 lb. thin roast beef slices
1 (8 oz.) jar soft processed cheese
6 (6 inch) French bread rolls, partially split and heated

Sauté onions in margarine, remove onions from skillet. Add meat to skillet, heat thoroughly, stirring occasionally.
Heat processed cheese spread in saucepan over low heat. Fill rolls with meat and onions.
Top with process cheese spread. Makes 6 sandwiches.

MALIBU CHICKEN SANDWICH

FOR 1:
1 breaded chicken breast, 3 oz. boneless
2 oz. shaved ham (very thin)
1 oz. 1 slice processed sliced Swiss cheese
1 hamburger bun

FOR 40:
40 breaded chicken breasts, 3 oz. boneless
5 lbs. shaved ham (very thin)
2 1/2 lbs. process sliced Swiss cheese
40 hamburger buns

Shave ham. Place in pan. Keep warm on grill (not hot). Cook the boneless chicken breast.
Place hot cooked chicken breast on bottom half of hamburger bun. Top chicken with ham, then a cheese slice.
Place in broiler 3 to 5 minutes until cheese starts to melt. Top with bun.
Serve immediately or wrap in foil and place in warmer.

MCMAHON SANDWICH

3/4 c. Miracle Whip salad dressing
2 tbsp. Kraft Pure Prepared Mustard
2 tbsp. dill pickle relish
1 Italian or French bread loaf, cut in half lengthwise
Shredded lettuce
Bologna slices
Salami slices
Turkey slices
Cucumber slices
Tomato slices
Onion rings
Kraft American Singles Pasteurized
Process Cheese Food

Combine salad dressing, mustard and relish; mix well. Spread bread loaf with salad dressing mixture; fill with remaining ingredients as desired. Yield: 6 to 8 servings.

MEATBALL SANDWICH

1-1/2 lb. hamburger
1 chopped onion
3/4 c. cracker crumbs
2 eggs
1 tsp. celery seed
Salt and pepper
1 jar spaghetti sauce
1/2 c. Parmesan cheese

Mix hamburger, onion, celery seed, eggs, cracker crumbs, Parmesan cheese and salt and pepper, real good.
Make into balls, put into flat baking pan. Put in oven at 450 degrees until brown.
Put into Dutch oven, pour spaghetti sauce, simmer for about 1 hour with lid on. Serve on buns.

MEAT & SLAW TAILGATE SANDWICH

1 1/2 lbs. savory cabbage, about 4 c. finely shredded
3/4 c. + 2 tbsp. mayonnaise
1 tbsp. Dijon
Salt & pepper
2 tomatoes
1 lg. round loaf crusty bread
1/2 lb. sliced ham
1/4 lb. sliced salami

Shred cabbage. Combine with 3/4 cup mayonnaise, the mustard, 1/4 teaspoon salt and 1/8 teaspoon pepper.
Slice tomatoes. Cut bread in two horizontally about 1" from the bottom. Pull out soft bread leaving top and bottom crust and a 1" rim around the circumference. Spread bottom of bread with remaining 2 tablespoons mayonnaise.
Cover with ham, salami and tomato slices. Pile coleslaw over tomatoes and cover with top of bread. Cut into 12 wedges to serve.

MEXICALI SANDWICH

1/2 c.	mayonnaise
1 (8 oz.) pkg.	cream cheese
6	hard-cooked eggs, chopped
1/4 c.	chopped green pepper
1 tbsp.	chopped onion
12 slices	whole wheat bread

Gradually add mayonnaise to softened cream cheese, mixing until well blended.

Add eggs, green pepper, and onion; mix well.

Makes 6 generously filled sandwiches.

MILE HIGH SHREDDED BEEF

3 lbs chuck roast or round steak
Vegetable oil
1 cup chopped onion
1/2 cup chopped celery
2 cups beef broth OR bouillon

Sauce:
1-1/2 cups beef broth reserved from roast
1 clove garlic, minced
1 teaspoon salt
3/4 teaspoon salt
4 tablespoons brown sugar
2 tablespoons vinegar
1 teaspoon dry mustard
1/2 teaspoon chili powder
3 drops Tabasco sauce
1 bay leaf
1/4 teaspoon paprika
1/4 teaspoon garlic powder
1 teaspoon Worcestershire sauce
Potato rolls or buns

Brown beef in hot oil on both sides, adding onion and celery at the
last minute. Combine beef, vegetables and broth in a Dutch oven or
crockpot. Simmer, covered, for 3-4 hours or until tender. Cool; shred
beef, separating into strands. Drain vegetables. Combine with beef.
Reserve broth; skim off any fat.

To make sauce: Mix broth, beef, vegetables, garlic, salt, catsup, brown
sugar, vinegar, mustard, chili powder, Tabasco, bay leaf, paprika, garlic
powder, and Worcestershire sauce. Simmer until heated thoroughly.

MONTE CARLO SANDWICHES

8 slices whole wheat bread, dry or old
4 slices ham, cooked
4 slices turkey breast, cooked
4 slices Swiss cheese
4 eggs, beaten
1/2 c. milk
1/4 tsp. salt

On each of four bread slices, place 1 slice each of ham, turkey and cheese.
Cover with remaining slices of bread. In a bowl, beat eggs, milk and salt together.
Dip each sandwich carefully into egg mixture, turning to dip each side.
Fry in sprayed or oiled pan like you would French toast, making sure cheese is melted and meat is hot.
May be put on sprayed cookie sheet; bake at 375 degrees, turning once.

NEW YORK SUBMARINE SANDWICHES

4 (6") or 2 (12") hoagie rolls
Olive oil
Red wine vinegar
Italian seasoning
12 slices provolone cheese
12 slices boiled ham
12 slices hard salami
2 sliced tomatoes
1/4-1/2 head shredded lettuce
1 sm. onion, sliced into thin rings

Split rolls. Sprinkle liberally with olive oil. Then vinegar and then the
Italian seasoning.
Layer 3 slices each of the provolone, ham and salami on each roll. (Or
6 each on the 12 inch rolls.)
Place sliced tomatoes, onions and shredded lettuce on top of cold cuts.
Slice 12 inch rolls in half to serve. Serves 4.

OPEN FACED HAWAIIAN SANDWICH

4 slices bread toasted
4 slices pineapples, drained
Miracle Whip
9-12 slices bacon, cooked & drained
4 slices white American cheese

Spread toast with Miracle Whip. Put pineapple on top of that. Put cooked bacon on top of pineapple and put white American cheese slice on top of bacon. Put on cookie sheet and cook until cheese is melted.
Bake at 350 degrees for 3-5 minutes.

OPEN FACED MEAT LOAF SANDWICHES

1 lb. ground chuck
1/3 c. chopped green pepper
1/3 c. chopped onion
1/3 c. soft bread crumbs
1/4 c. skim milk
1 egg, beaten
1 tbsp. reduced calorie catsup
1/4 tsp. garlic powder
1/4 tsp. salt or Papa Dash
1/4 tsp. pepper
Vegetable cooking spray
1 (8 oz.) can no salt added tomato sauce
1/4 tsp. dried whole oregano
1/4 tsp. dried whole marjoram
6 (1/2 inch thick) slices Italian bread, toasted

Combine first 10 ingredients in a medium bowl; stir well. Spoon mixture into a 7 1/2 x 3 x 2 inch loaf pan that has been coated with cooking spray. Bake at 350 degrees for 1 hour and 10 minutes.

Cool in pan 5 minutes. Remove from pan; drain well on paper towels. Let stand 5 minutes before cutting into 1 inch slices. Combine tomato sauce, oregano, and marjoram in a small saucepan. Bring mixture to a boil.

Cover; reduce heat, and simmer 10 minutes, stirring occasionally. Place toasted bread slices on serving platter.
Top each slice with a meatloaf slice. Spoon 2 tablespoon tomato sauce over each sandwich.

ORTEGA SANDWICHES

Leftover roast or steak
6 hard cooked eggs
1 can chopped ripe olives
1 can (10 oz.) tomato sauce
6 oz. oil
Salt, pepper, garlic salt
1 1/2 c. mild Cheddar cheese, shredded
1 (7 oz.) can chopped green chilies
2 to 3 jalapenos, chopped
Hard rolls

Grind meat. Chop eggs and olives and shred cheese. Mix all
ingredients together well.
Put mixture on hard rolls and wrap each roll in foil and freeze. When
ready to eat, heat rolls in oven for 15 minutes at 350 degrees.
You can make these as mild or as hot as you want. Good for lunches,
camping or just a hot snack.

POLISH SANDWICHES

1 lb. ground beef
1/2 c. chopped onion
1/2 c. chopped green pepper
2 tbsp. margarine
1 jar beef gravy
2 c. shredded cabbage
1/2 c. shredded cheddar cheese

In skillet, brown meat and cook onions and green peppers in margarine until tender. Stir in gravy and cabbage.
Cook over medium heat until cabbage is tender. Serve on rolls and top with cheese. Salt and pepper may be added.

PORK SANDWICH (THE MIKADO)

3 lbs. boneless pork roast or tenderloin, cooked
1/2 c. applesauce
5 tbsp. honey
5 tbsp. prepared mustard
2 eggs, beaten
1 tbsp. soy sauce
1/4 tsp. garlic powder
1/4 tsp. poultry seasoning
1/2 tsp. salt
1/4 tsp. pepper
3/4 c. bread crumbs
1/4 c. sesame seed
1/2 tsp. seasoned salt
Butter or Lard for browning
12 English muffins, split, toasted
Butter
Lettuce leaves

Slit 12 (2 oz.) slices from a double pork loin roast or 24 (1 oz.) slices from a single pork roast.
Combine applesauce, mustard and honey; chill. Blend beaten eggs, soy sauce, garlic powder, poultry seasoning, salt and pepper. Combine bread crumbs, sesame seed and seasoned salt.
Dip pork slices in egg mixture and coat with crumb mixture. Brown on both sides in butter on a grill.
Butter toasted English muffins. Place lettuce leaf on one half of each muffin and top with 2 ounces breaded pork slices. Spread applesauce mixture (approximately 1 tablespoon) on each of remaining muffin halves.
Serve open faced or close for eating, if desired. Yield: 12 servings.

QUICK (KULWIK) SANDWICHES

1/4 c. prepared pizza sauce
8 slices Italian bread, cut diagonally 3/4 inch thick)
1/2 lb. thinly sliced Mozzarella cheese
1/4 lb. thinly sliced baked ham
1 egg
2 tbsp. butter or margarine

Spread 1 tablespoon pizza sauce on each of 4 bread slices; layer on top Mozzarella.
Place ham on Mozzarella. In small bowl, beat egg with 1 tablespoons water.
Dip both sides of sandwiches in egg mixture. Coat entirely. Melt butter in large skillet over medium heat.
Place sandwiches in skillet; cook for 5 minutes or until lightly browned. Turn once.

REUBEN SANDWICH

8 slices pumpernickel or dark bread
1/2 lb. thinly sliced corned beef
1 (8 oz.) can well drained sauerkraut
2 tbsp. Thousand Island dressing or mayonnaise
4 sliced Swiss cheese

Spread all slices of bread with mayonnaise or dressing. Then, on 4
slices, add sauerkraut, sliced corned beef, and a piece of cheese.
Top with other slices of bread. Lightly butter the outside of the bread
and grill or toast on a grill or griddle uncovered 3 to 3 1/2 minutes,
or until cheese is melted and bread is brown. Serve immediately.

RUSSIAN SANDWICH

1 slice rye bread
1 slice baked ham
1 slice Swiss/Provolone cheese
1 slice white turkey; optional
3 slices tomatoes

On each individual plate, build each sandwich in above order. Pour dressing over each sandwich; sprinkle bacon bits; garnish with wedges of hard boiled eggs, carrot strips, olives, or lettuce.

DRESSING:
1 bottle Heinz chili sauce
10 oz. Heinz pickle relish
1 pt. mayonnaise

Mix all together well and pour over open face sandwiches. May be stored in refrigerator for future use.

SALMON SALAD COUNTRY CLUB SANDWICH

24 slices white sandwich bread, trimmed slightly

SALMON SALAD FILLING:
16 oz. canned red salmon, drained, skinned, flaked & deboned
1/4 c. pimiento
1/4 c. green pepper, minced
1 tsp. onion, grated
1/4 c. Miracle Whip
Mix all ingredients together; set aside.

SPINACH SALAD FILLING:
16 oz. soft cream cheese
1/2 c. chopped parsley
1/2 c. minced fresh spinach
2 tbsp. milk
2 drops hot pepper sauce
Mix all ingredients together; set aside.

EGG SALAD FILLING:
6 eggs, hard cooked, chopped
1/2 c. celery, minced fine
1 tsp. grated onion
1/2 c. Miracle Whip
Season to taste

Mix all ingredients together; set aside. Spread 4 slices of bread with
Miracle Whip for each sandwich.
Line with lettuce and stack 3 different salads on 3 slices of bread and
top with remaining slice of bread.
Cut diagonally, and place on plate and serve. Tomato slices, gherkins
and potato chips make a good accompaniment.
Yield: 6 servings.

SAUSAGE ON RYE SLICES

1 lb. hot sausage
1 lb. lean ground beef
1 lb. Velveeta cheese
1 tbsp. Worcestershire sauce
Salt and pepper
3 loaves cocktail rye slices

Fry sausage with beef. Drain drippings. Add cheese, oregano, Worcestershire sauce.
Add salt and pepper to taste. Stir until cheese meets. Spread on rye slices.

SEBASTIAN SANDWICH

12 slices rye bread
Butter or oleo
2/3 c. mayonnaise
1/3 c. chopped chutney
1 tbsp. curry powder
1 tsp. salt
3 c. shredded cabbage
1 lb. sliced baked ham
6 slices cheddar cheese

Butter both sides of bread. Combine mayonnaise, chutney, curry powder and salt; fold in cabbage.
On each of 6 slices of bread, place equal amounts of sliced ham, about 1/2 cup cabbage mixture and 1 slice cheese.
Top with remaining bread slices. Grill both sides until golden brown.

6 sandwiches.

SEVEN LAYER TACO SANDWICH

1/2 c. coarsely chopped ripe olives
1/2 tsp. chili powder
1/2 tsp. ground cumin
1/4 tsp. salt
1/2 c. mayonnaise
1/2 c. sour cream
1/2 c. sliced green onion
4 lg. oval slices French bread (about
1/2" thick)
1 lg. tomato, sliced
1 lb. thinly sliced roasted deli turkey breast
1 ripe avocado, peeled, seeded & sliced
3/4 c. shredded cheddar cheese
3/4 c. shredded Monterey Jack cheese
Lettuce leaves
Salsa

Combine olives, chili powder, cumin and salt in medium bowl; reserve 2 tablespoons.
Stir mayonnaise, sour cream and onion into remaining olive mixture.
Spread one side of each bread slice with half the mayonnaise mixture. Top with tomato and turkey.
Spread remaining mayonnaise mixture on top of turkey. Top with avocado slices. Sprinkle with cheese.
Transfer sandwiches to baking sheet. Bake at 350 degrees until heated through, about 15 minutes.
Top with reserved olive mixture. Serve sandwiches on lettuce leaves with salsa. Yield: 4 servings.

SNAPPY HAM SANDWICHES

2 cans (2 1/4 oz. each) deviled ham
2 lg. English muffins, cut in halves
1 (3 oz.) pkg. cream cheese
1/4 c. finely chopped onion
1/4 c. chopped stuffed olives
4 thin tomato slices
Mayonnaise

Toast cut side of each muffin in broiler. Combine cream cheese, onion and olives.
Spread mixture on toasted side of each muffin half. Spread deviled ham over cream cheese mixture.
Top each sandwich with a tomato slice. Spread tomato slice lightly with mayonnaise. Place under broiler until heated through. (4 sandwiches.)

STROGANOFF STEAK SANDWICH

2/3 c. beer
1/3 c. cooking oil
1 tsp. salt
1/4 tsp. garlic powder
1/4 tsp. pepper
2 lb. flank steak, about 1 inch thick
2 tbsp. butter or margarine
1/2 tsp. paprika
4 c. sliced onion
12 slices French bread, toasted
1 c. dairy sour cream, warmed
1/2 tsp. prepared horseradish

In shallow dish, combine beer, oil, salt, garlic powder and pepper.
Place flank steak in marinade; cover.
Marinate overnight in refrigerator or several hours at room
temperature; drain.
Broil flank steak 3 inches from heat for 5 to 7 minutes on each side for
medium rare.
In saucepan, melt butter or margarine; blend in paprika and a dash of
salt. Add onion; cook until tender but not brown.
Thinly slice meat on the diagonal across grain. For each serving
arrange meat slices of 2 slices French bread.
Top with onions. Combine sour cream and horseradish; spoon onto
each sandwich. Sprinkle with paprika. Makes 6 servings.

STROMBOLI HOT ITALIAN SANDWICH

1 lb. frozen bread dough, defrosted and rolled into a rectangle
1 layer sliced salami, placed down center of dough full length
1 layer ham, placed as above
1 layer Mozzarella cheese, placed as above
1 egg

Season layers with pepper, oregano and olive oil to taste. Roll up; tuck in ends.
Brush with beaten egg and sprinkle with Parmesan cheese.

Bake at 375 degrees about 20 minutes or until brown. Let cool slightly. Slice and serve warm.

STROMBOLI SANDWICHES

1 lb. ground beef
1 onion, chopped
1/2 c. ketchup
2 tsp. Parmesan cheese
1/2 c. tomato sauce
1/4 tsp. garlic powder
1/4 tsp. margarine
1/4 tsp. oregano
Sliced Mozzarella cheese

Brown ground beef. Add all other ingredients except Mozzarella cheese. Simmer for 20 minutes.
Spoon mixture onto hamburger buns. Put a slice of Mozzarella cheese on top of ground beef and seal in foil.
Bake in oven at 350 degrees for 15 minutes.

STUFFED SANDWICH TO GO

1 8 oz. cream cheese
1/4 c. finely chopped green onion
1/4 c. finely chopped walnuts
1/4 tsp. garlic powder
1 loaf unsliced French Vienna 12" x
5" bread
1/4 lb. fresh spinach
1/2 lb. Swiss cheese
1/2 c. alfalfa sprouts
Butter
3/4 lb. boiled ham, sliced thin
Heavy duty foil, enough to wrap loaf.

Stir together cream cheese, walnuts, green onion and garlic. Set aside.
With serrated knife, slice top off the bread.
Cut down around loaf edge about 1/2" from the side and bottom
crust. With a fork pull out the center of the bread.
Butter the cavity and top slice, line the cavity with ham so that slice
overlaps sides. Top with half the spinach then half the Swiss cheese.
Spread cream cheese mixture over Swiss cheese layer. Top with alfalfa
sprouts, the remaining Swiss cheese and remaining spinach.
Fold the ends of ham over spinach to cover top. Wrap bread in foil.
Chill several hours. Slice and serve.

SUPER BOWL SUBS

1 loaf (16 inches long) Italian bread
1 med. avocado, mashed
1 tbsp. lemon juice
1 tbsp. mayonnaise
1/2 tsp. salt
1/4 tsp. hot pepper sauce
1 clove garlic, minced
8 oz. cooked turkey meat
7 oz. sliced Monterey Jack cheese
2 med. tomatoes, sliced
1/4 c. chopped scallion
1 (4 oz.) can sliced green chilies, drained and cut into strips
12 pitted ripe olives, sliced (optional)

Halve bread lengthwise and crosswise to make quarters. Place 2 bread pieces on oven pan of toaster oven.
Toast, watching carefully to avoid over browning. Repeat with rest of bread.
In a small bowl, mash avocado with lemon juice, mayonnaise, salt, pepper sauce and garlic.
Spread 1/4 of mixture on toasted bread surface. Layer 1/4 of turkey, cheese, tomato and onion over top of each.
Top with chilies. Place 2 sandwiches on oven pan of toaster oven and brown until cheese is bubbly. Repeat with remaining sandwiches.
Serve hot, garnished with olives.

SUPER DUPER SANDWICHES

3 English muffins, split and toasted
3 tbsp. butter or margarine
1 lg. tomato cut in 6 slices
1 can (6 1/2 oz) tuna, drained and flaked
2 tbsp. mayonnaise
3 slices cheddar or Swiss cheese

Spread muffins with butter. Arrange in circle on large paper towel-lined microwave proof plate.
Place tomato slice on each muffin. Mix tuna and mayonnaise until blended. Divide and spoon tuna over tomato slices.
Cut cheese diagonally in half to form triangles. Place 1 triangle of cheese on each muffin.
Use "defrost" cycle and cook 7 to 8 minutes or until cheese melts and muffin topping is warm.
Let stand 2 minutes before serving. A single split muffin can be prepared and cooked on "defrost" cycle for 1 to 1 1/2 minutes.
Toasted bread can be substituted for English muffins.

SUPER HAM SANDWICHES

1 stick margarine
1/4 c. mustard
1/4 c. minced onion
1 lb. shaved deli ham
1 lb. Mozzarella cheese, sliced
3 pans ready to serve finger rolls

Saute onion in margarine. Add mustard. Split each pan of rolls and brush both sides with mixture. Layer on cheese and ham.
Return to roll pan and cover with foil. Heat in 350 degree oven until cheese is melted. Cut into individual sandwiches.

SYMPHONY SANDWICHES

1	tablespoon	Dijon mustard
1	tablespoon	reduced-fat mayonnaise
1/8	teaspoon	garlic powder
1/2		California avocado -- optional
1	medium	tomato
2		flavored 10-inch flour tortillas -- (wraps)
1/4	pound	smoked deli turkey
4	slices	provolone cheese
1/2	cup	shredded carrots
1/2	cup	alfalfa sprouts

In a small dish, stir together the mustard, mayonnaise and garlic powder.
If using the avocado, cut it in half and twist to remove the seed. Reserve one half for another use. Cut the remaining half in half. Peel the skin away from the flesh. Cut each piece into 4 slices and set aside. Slice the unpeeled tomato and set aside.

Microwave the first tortilla for 30 seconds, uncovered, on high. Spread half the mustard mixture over the entire tortilla surface. In the center of the tortilla, leaving a 1/2-inch edge, place 2 slices of cheese and half each of the turkey, avocado (if using), tomato, carrots and sprouts. Fold in the sides and roll it up burrito-style.

Repeat the process to make the second sandwich.

Cut the sandwiches in half and wrap each half in foil. Serve at once or refrigerate until ready to serve.

TERIYAKI SLOW COOK SANDWICHES

2 - 2 1/2 lbs. boneless beef chuck steak
1/4 c. soy sauce
1 tbsp. brown sugar
1 tsp. ground ginger
1 clove garlic, minced
4 tsp. cornstarch
8 individual French loaves, split
4 tbsp. margarine or butter, melted

TOPPINGS: Such as shredded Chinese cabbage, pineapple rings, sliced green onion, plum sauce or sweet and sour sauce (optional). Trim excess fat from steak; cut into thin, bite size slices. In a 3 1/2 to 4 quart crockery cooker, combine soy sauce, brown sugar, ginger and garlic. Stir in meat. Cover; cook on low heat setting for 7 to 9 hours or high heat setting for 3 to 4 hours.

Remove meat from juices with a slotted spoon. Pour juices into a measuring cup; skim fat from cooking juices.
Measure 1 1/2 cups juices (add water if necessary) and place in a saucepan.

Combine cornstarch and 2 tablespoons water; add to saucepan. Cook and stir until thickened and bubbly.
Stir in cooked meat. Heat through. Meanwhile, brush rolls lightly with margarine or butter.

Place on unheated rack of broiler pan. Broil, cut side up, 4" to 5" from heat for 2 or 3 minutes or until lightly toasted.
Top bottom halves of the toasted rolls with meat mixture and desired toppings. Cover with roll tops. Makes 8 servings.

TEX - MEX BURGERS

1 1/2 lb. ground beef
1 (4 oz.) can green chilies, drained and chopped
3 oz. jack cheese, cut into 1/4" cubes
6 hamburger buns
6 tbsp. sour cream
6 tbsp. salsa
6 lettuce leaves (optional)

Heat grill or skillet. Shape ground beef into twelve 3 1/2" patties.
Place six patties on waxed paper.
Top each one with 1/6 of the chilies and cheese. Place remaining
patties over stuffing. Press edges to seal.
Grill or fry until burgers are done. Serve on buns with sour cream,
salsa and lettuce.

TRIPLE-DECKER SANDWICH

Mayonnaise
Honey mustard or 1000 Island dressing
Rye bread
Lettuce
Sm. tomato
Swiss cheese
Cheddar cheese
Sliced baked ham
Sliced turkey

Generously coat one side of three slices of bread with mayonnaise, 1000 Island dressing or honey-mustard.
Then alternate bread, lettuce, tomato, sliced baked ham, Swiss cheese, sliced turkey and Cheddar cheese to build sandwich.

TUNA PUFF SANDWICH

1 (7 oz.) can tuna, flaked
1 1/2 tsp. prepared mustard
1/4 tsp. Worcestershire sauce
1/4 c. Hellmann's mayonnaise
1 1/2 tsp. grated onion
2 tbsp. green pepper, chopped
3 hamburger rolls, split
6 slices tomatoes
1/2 c. mayonnaise
1/4 c. grated or shredded cheese or slices will do

Blend first 6 ingredients. Pile onto bun halves. Top each with tomato slices. Blend 1/2 the mayonnaise with cheese
and spread on tomato slice. Broil 4 inches from heat, until topping browns and puffs. Takes a few minutes.

TURKEY 'N CHIVE SANDWICH

8 oz. pkg. cream cheese, softened
2 tbsp. chopped fresh chives
4 individual French bread rolls, split
4 lettuce leaves
8 slices cooked turkey
1 med. sliced tomato
1 med. sliced green pepper
4 slices Swiss cheese

Combine cream cheese and chives, spread on roll halves. To make sandwiches layer lettuce leaf,
2 slices turkey, tomato, green pepper and 1 slice cheese.

TURKEY SANDWICHES

8 slices whole wheat or rye bread
Reduced calorie salad dressing
1 med. onion, thinly sliced, red or white
4 oz. fresh mushrooms, sliced
Lettuce leaves
12 oz. shaved turkey

Lightly spread bread with salad dressing. Using 1 teaspoon oil, saute onion and then mushrooms; cook until tender. Layer with turkey slices, onion and mushroom mixture, lettuce and top with remaining slices of bread. Open face sandwiches can be made by layering turkey, onion and mushroom mixture and then topped by slice of Mozzarella cheese. Heat in toaster oven or broiler until cheese begins to melt and slightly browned.

TURKEY WALDORF SANDWICH

1 c. turkey, cooked, trimmed, bones removed, cut into 1/2 inch cubes
1/2 c. celery, washed, ends removed, diced
1 sm. Red Delicious apple, washed, cored, and cut into small cubes
2 tbsp. shelled walnuts, chopped
1 tbsp. reduced-calorie mayonnaise or salad dressing
1 tbsp. non-fat yogurt
1/8 tsp. nutmeg
1/8 tsp. cinnamon
4 lettuce leaves, washed, dried
8 slices reduced-calorie raisin bread

In a medium size bowl, combine turkey, celery, apple, walnuts,
mayonnaise, yogurt, nutmeg and cinnamon.
Cover and refrigerate at least 1 hour or overnight to allow flavors to
blend. To serve, arrange one lettuce leaf on one slice of bread.
Spoon 3/4 cup turkey mixture over lettuce leaf and top with another
bread slice.
Repeat with remaining mixture, lettuce leaves and bread. Serves 4.

WEST POINT SANDWICH

Ready to bake rolls in aluminum pan
6 oz. pkg. slices Swiss cheese
8-9 oz. pkg. thin sliced ham
1 stick margarine
2 tbsp. grated onion
3 tbsp. mustard
2 tbsp. Worcestershire sauce
2 tbsp. poppy seeds

Turn rolls out of pan but do not separate. Slice through middle of rolls
and set top aside.
Mix all ingredients except ham and Swiss cheese. Spread on top and
bottom of bread.
Arrange ham and cheese on bottom half. Replace top half. Put back in
pan and cover with foil.
Bake at 350 degrees for 30 minutes. Serve hot.

65186024R00064

Made in the USA
Lexington, KY
03 July 2017